OIL PROCESSING

Food Cycle Technology Source Books

OIL PROCESSING

Practical Action Publishing Ltd
27a Albert Street, Rugby, CV21 2SG, Warwickshire, UK
www.practicalactionpublishing.org

First published as Oil Extraction by UNIFEM in 1987
This edition published 1993

Transferred to digital printing in 2008

ISBN 13: 978 1 85339 134 7
ISBN PDF: 9781780444192

A catalogue record for this book is available from the British Library.

Since 1974, Practical Action Publishing has published and disseminated books and information in support of international development work throughout the world. Practical Action Publishing is a trading name of Practical Action Publishing Ltd (Company Reg. No. 1159018), the wholly owned publishing company of Practical Action. Practical Action Publishing trades only in support of its parent charity objectives and any profits are covenanted back to Practical Action (Charity Reg. No. 247257, Group VAT Registration No. 880 9924 76).

Illustrations by Peter Dobson
Typeset by Inforum, Rowlands Castle, Hants, UK

Preface

This source book is one of a continuing UNIFEM series which aims to increase awareness of the range of technological options and sources of expertise, as well as indicating the complexity of designing and successfully implementing technology development and dissemination programmes.

UNIFEM was established in 1976, and is an autonomous body associated since 1984 with the United Nations Development Programme. UNIFEM seeks to free women from under-productive tasks and augment the productivity of their work as a means of accelerating the development process. It does this through funding specific women's projects which yield direct benefits and through actions directed to ensure that all development policies, plans, programmes and projects take account of the needs of women producers.

In recognition of women's special roles in the production, processing, storage, preparation and marketing of food, UNIFEM initiated a Food Cycle Technology project in 1985 with the aim of promoting the widespread diffusion of tested technologies to increase the productivity of women's labour in this sector. While global in perspective, the initial phase of the project was implemented in Africa in view of the concern over food security in many countries of the region.

A careful evaluation of the Africa experience in the final phase of this five-year programme showed that there was a need for catalytic interventions which would lead to an enabling environment for women to have easier access to technologies. This would be an environment where women producers can obtain information on the available technologies, have the capacity to analyse such information, make technological choices on their own, and acquire credit and training to enable the purchase and operation of the technology of their choice. This UNIFEM source book series aims to facilitate the building of such an environment.

Acknowledgements

This series of food cycle technology source books has been prepared at the Intermediate Technology Development Group (ITDG) in the United Kingdom within the context of UNIFEM's Women and Food Cycle Technologies (WAFT) specialization.

During the preparation process the project staff contacted numerous project directors, rural development agencies, technology centres, women's organizations, equipment manufacturers and researchers in all parts of the world.

The authors wish to thank the many agencies and individuals who have contributed to the preparation of this source book. Special thanks are owed to the International Labour Organization (ILO), the Food and Agriculture Organization of the United Nations (FAO), the United Nations Children's Fund (UNICEF), the Economic Commission for Africa (ECA), the German Appropriate Technology Exchange (GATE/GTZ) in Eschborn, the Groupe de Recherche et d'Echanges Technologiques (GRET) in Paris, the Royal Tropical Institute (KIT) in Amsterdam, the International Development Research Centre (IDRC) in Ottawa, the Natural Resources Institute (NRI) in Chatham, Appropriate Technologies International (ATI) in Washington, the Institute of Development Studies (IDS) at Sussex University, and the Save the Children Fund.

The preparation of the source books was funded by UNIFEM with a cost-sharing contribution from the Government of Italy and the Government of the Netherlands. UNIFEM is also grateful to the Government of Italy, via the Italian Association of Women in Development (AIDOS), for sponsoring the translation of this series into French and Portuguese, and the printing of the first editions.

Barrie Axtell
IT Consultants

Els Kocken
UNIFEM

Ruby Sandhu
UNIFEM

Contents

Contents

Introduction

THIS SOURCE BOOK is designed for people who have little or no technical background or previous knowledge of oil extraction and processing. It provides a basic introduction to both traditional and improved methods. Comparisons are made between different improved technologies. Only those oil-seeds, nuts, and fruits which are widely processed using traditional methods are discussed. There are several other oil-bearing raw materials which are not covered in this book because they either require more sophisticated technology for oil extraction or are not commonly used. As some oil-bearing materials such as Kapok are toxic, any unusual oil-seed should be investigated individually and treated with caution.

Throughout the book, specific points or warnings are made about particular processes or products. For example, it is mentioned that castor seed contains toxic substances and that oil extracted from it by traditional methods would be harmful for medicinal uses. Attention must be paid to these warnings.

Descriptions and comparisons of the various technologies aim to show under what circumstances they may be technically appropriate or inappropriate. More importantly, the technology may prove to be appropriate or inappropriate for social, economic, cultural, or environmental reasons. Introduction of any new processing system to rural areas requires a thorough understanding of the socio-economic and cultural relations of the users. Socio-economic research needs to be conducted alongside technical research if technologies which seem to be applicable, relevant, and acceptable are to be introduced. Manual oil processing is usually done by women, and attention should be paid not only to identifying the wants, needs, and problems of rural women, but also to the possible consequences for women and other users.

Careful and strategic planning, such as the provision of training through extension workers in the use and maintenance of equipment, is required in order to make new or improved technologies understood and accessible to the rural women. Successful use of any technology also depends upon infrastructural support and services. The users should be able to maintain and replace parts using locally available resources and skills at an affordable price.

Economic factors are often a constraint. Women are frequently denied access to formal lines of credit because they cannot provide any collateral and they usually do not have access to advice on how to obtain loans on an individual, group or co-operative basis. In some cases, because of the existing social structure, mere formation of co-operatives may prove to be problematic. In formulating any project, careful and thorough consideration of the socio-economic issues is essential for long-term sustainability. Planning includes defining motivation, management, administration, organization of the participants, training, credit, and so on. The organization of women participants in the project in terms of roles, responsibilities, anticipated benefits and payback should be explicit, and put into the context of the women's own expectations.

These organizational issues are usually more difficult to resolve than technical problems and unfortunately are often not given sufficient attention. Each project must be designed and adapted according to local socio-economic conditions and needs. Introductory questions useful in the planning processes are to be found in the checklist in Section 5.

Additionally, attention should be addressed to the control of resources and existing market mechanisms. Women would need, for example, access to raw materials if a greater demand was created through the introduction of a technology.

All the above points are raised in greater detail in the case studies and the checklist of questions. It is always important to keep in mind that any improvement needs to be more than just technically feasible.

1
Raw materials from which oil can be extracted

THIS SECTION lists selected seeds, nuts and fruits from which oil can be extracted and is restricted to those materials that are processed traditionally on a wide scale. (TPI, 1971)

Raw material	Oil content	Use
Oil-seeds		
Castor	35–55%	Paints, lubricants*
Cotton	15–25%	Cooking oil, soap-making
Linseed	35–44%	Paints, varnishes
Niger	38–50%	Cooking oil, soap, paint
Neem	45% of kernel	Soap-making
Rape/mustard	40–45%	Cooking oil
Sesame	35–50%	Cooking oil
Sunflower	25–40%	Cooking oil, soap-making
Nuts		
Coconuts	64% dried copra 35% fresh nut	Cooking oil, body/hair cream, soap-making
Groundnuts	38–50%	Cooking oil, soap-making
Palm kernel nuts	46–57%	Cooking oil, body/hair cream, soap-making
Shea-nut	34–44%	Cooking oil, soap-making
Mesocarps		
Oil palm (wet)	56%	Cooking oil, soap-making

* Only castor oil which has been processed using sophisticated technology can be used for medicinal purposes.

2
Traditional methods of oil extraction

BEFORE attempts are made to introduce improved methods of oil extraction, an effort should be made to understand the traditional methods employed. As will be seen from the case studies, technologies which are not based on a good understanding of traditional processing tend to have a low acceptance rate.

This section seeks to outline the various steps involved in traditional methods of processing. As these differ somewhat from place to place it would not be feasible to record all the minor variations that occur. Therefore, examples are given of fairly standard processing methods which can serve as a basis for comparison with the system used in any particular area.

This section is divided into:
Oil-seeds (sunflower, sesame, mustard, and so on)
Nuts: ○ groundnuts (peanuts)
　　　○ palm kernel nuts
　　　○ coconuts
　　　○ shea-nuts
Mesocarps (palm fruit)

Oil-seed processing

Oil-seeds (sunflower, sesame, etc.) are still commonly processed using traditional methods which are usually time-consuming and strenuous. In most cases, seeds are ground to a paste without removing the husk or outer covering. In some instances sunflower seeds are husked. Seeds are ground manually unless a local mill is both accessible and affordable. The paste is heated, alone at first, and then with boiling water. The mixture is stirred and brought to the boil. After boiling, the mixture is allowed to cool during which time the oil gathers at the top and is scooped off. In traditional methods of processing oil-seeds the extraction efficiency is about 40 per cent (extraction efficiency refers to the percentage of oil extract based on the total theoretical content, which of course is never in practice obtained) (NRI, unpublished information). In parts of Asia, oil-seeds are traditionally processed using ghanis which are described in greater detail in the section covering improved methods.

Nuts

Processing methods of different oil-bearing nuts are discussed separately as the procedures vary somewhat.

Groundnuts

The production of groundnut oil and its by-products, raw and fried cake, is an important source of income for women in large areas of Africa. A typical process from West Africa is as follows, although there may be regional variations.

The groundnuts are first shelled and then grilled which is very time-consuming; for example, 30 kg of groundnuts requires four to five hours. The grilled nuts are skinned by placing them on a mat and rolling a wooden block over them, or by rolling them under a stick and then winnowing them. The skinned nuts are then either ground to a paste using a pestle and mortar or head-loaded to a local mill. Boiling water is added and the mixture is stirred until the oil separates from the paste. The oil is scooped off the surface and heated in order to boil off any remaining water.

At the household level this whole process could take about four hours, not including the time spent travelling to and from the mill. The remaining cake may be formed into balls which are sold to be used in the preparation of groundnut soup or fried and sold as a snack food (Corbett, S., 1981).

Palm kernel nuts

Nuts of palm oil fruits are also an important source of oil. After they have been cracked open manually, the nuts are grilled over an open fire, using sheet metal pans, iron pots, or earthenware pots. Grilling takes between one and four hours. The cracking of the palm kernel nut is the most tedious part of the process, and wastage through poor separation of nut and shell can be as high as 50–60 per cent.

The grilled nuts are pounded in a mortar or milled mechanically and then boiled with water. Finally, oil is scooped off the top of the boiling mixture. This process takes one to two hours. The residue can be used for animal feed (ITDG, unpublished information).

Coconuts

There are three basic ways of extracting oil from coconut meat and these are used mostly in Asia. The most common one is the cooking method where fresh coconut meat is grated by hand, then mixed with warm water and squeezed by hand or pressed by foot at least three times. A milky-looking liquid emulsion is obtained and allowed to settle for three hours to separate the cream from the water. The cream is then scooped off or, alternatively, the water at the bottom is siphoned out. It is then boiled in a pan until the moisture has evaporated and a mixture of oil and coagulated protein remains. The oil is separated by straining the mixture when cooled.

The second method is to dry the coconut meat into copra which is later milled or ground. The ground copra is pressed in wooden presses using the principle of leverage to separate the oil from the copra meal.

The third, less widely practised process, is the fermentation method. Coconut milk from grated coconut is allowed to stand for two to three days by which time oil appears on the surface of the milk.

Traditionally prepared coconut oil tends, because of the presence of traces of water in it, to develop rancidity and thus cannot be stored for very long. Using the above methods, on average the yield of oil from 300 nuts is about 25 litres. The remaining residue – copra meal or coagulated protein – can be used as a constituent of animal feed or in food (FAO, 1968).

Shea-nuts

Shea-butter processing provides approximately 60 per cent of the cash income for women in the Sahel, and is a vital source of fat in the community. (The distinction between an oil and a fat is simply that at normal temperatures oils are liquid and fats solid.) Women are often obliged to sell the unprocessed shea-nuts to factories at low prices because of their urgent cash needs and the demands on their labour during the farming season.

The outside pulp of the berries, the shea-fruit, is eaten at harvest time. The nuts are later dried, pounded, and ground in wooden mortars to a paste. It is essential that the paste is kept heated throughout the extraction process because shea-butter solidifies at 25 to 30°C.

Once the nuts are ground, the paste is heated until it becomes soft and is re-milled or, if no mill is available, kneaded manually. The product is then mixed with warm water and stirred vigorously to break the emulsion and separate the fat. The oil floats to the surface and is then skimmed off. Despite the great labour involved, the extraction rates of oil are exceedingly low, about 15 per cent (Fleury, J.M., 1981).

Mesocarps

Traditional processing of palm fruit and other mesocarps is commonly carried out by women. The traditional method used is time-consuming, arduous, and inefficient. While details may vary from country to country, the methods are generally divided into two types, the 'hard oil' and 'soft oil' processes.

In the hard oil process, also referred to as the fermentation process, the bunches – usually broken up to some degree – are placed in disused canoes, especially constructed wooden troughs, or occasionally in clay-lined pits. The fruit is covered with water and allowed to ferment for several days through the action of naturally occurring fungi, yeasts, and enzymes in the fruit. The oil gradually rises to the surface of the water as the fruit decays and is skimmed off at regular intervals. It is usually boiled to remove water and often filtered through basketwork to remove any extraneous matter.

The process is inefficient in terms of oil yield, only about 20 to 30 per cent of the oil present being recovered. This is called the hard oil process because the oil contains a high percentage of free fatty acids (FFA) which result from the breakdown of the oil giving it an unpalatable and rancid flavour. Oil which has less than 7 per cent FFA is generally preferred for cooking purposes whereas oil produced through the fermentation method is used for soap-making, typically having an FFA content of 10 to 20 per cent (TDRI, 1984).

The soft oil process involves boiling the fruit after separating it from the bunches. It is then pounded in wooden mortars with pestles until a mass containing oil, fibre, and unbroken nuts is obtained. After kneading, the mass is sieved to remove unbroken nuts and fibres. The liquid mixture must be boiled to break down the oil and water emulsion. Oil then floats to the surface and is skimmed off with a calabash. This process yields an oil with a lower FFA content which is acceptable for food use (TDRI, 1984).

These traditional methods of palm oil production have an extraction efficiency of under 50 per cent and are both labour-intensive and time-consuming. Palm oil is a major source of edible oil and also of carotenes (vitamin A precursors) (ECA, 1983).

Women and oil extraction technologies

Fats and oils are critical to the well-being of many rural communities as a source of concentrated energy. The production of fats and oils provides an important source of income for women, not only in the direct production of oil but also through secondary products, for example soaps, snack foods and cosmetics.

Often, however, only the better-off can afford the time, credit, and fuel needed for processing. Poorer women may sell the raw materials for instant cash in times of need.

The major problem perceived by many women in traditional oil processing is the tiring nature of the work. Moreover, the establishment of large modern mills is presenting a threat to women's incomes. For example, in Nigeria, the introduction of modern power-driven palm oil mills resulted in women demonstrating against them because the whole palm fruit now went to the mill and the husbands received the money for the oil directly. This deprived the women of their income from palm 'kernel' oil which traditionally was the woman's personal reward for making palm oil. This also denied the family the income from the palm oil, as the men tended to keep the money from the sale of the palm fruit for themselves.

In order for women to compete with the large mills it is crucial that they have access to improved oil extraction technologies. This would add to their income and relieve them of some of their arduous tasks. Formal credit and other support services would help them process raw material (rather than sell it for instant cash) and thus generate a greater income.

In some cases, the price of oil does not give sufficient market return to pay for all the labour and capital that goes into its extraction. In many cases the profit comes from the production of the secondary, higher-value product. Women should be made aware of the potential value of by-products such as fibres and residues to make, for example, briquettes or animal feeds and not rely solely on extracted oil.

3
Improved technologies

IMPROVED TECHNOLOGIES exist for the small-scale processing of all types of oil-bearing raw materials both at the pre-processing and oil extraction stages. Broadly speaking, extraction devices fall into three categories: expellers, ghanis, and plate presses. These types are described on pages 7–9.

Expellers and ghanis are normally used for seeds and nuts because of the greater pressure that is required to extract oil from them. Screw-operated plate presses are used for extracting oil from mesocarps and groundnuts but hydraulic presses, because they generate high pressure, are able to process seeds and nuts. Some materials require a pre-processing stage prior to oil extraction and this section discusses both the pre-processing steps and the various oil extraction devices.

Where appropriate, information is included on the possibility of local manufacture. This is important because it gives an idea of the scale of workshop that would be needed to produce equipment. Since skills and resources differ from region to region it is important to find out what resources exist and judge what equipment can be made.

It is important to highlight further the implications of the term 'local availability'. Generally, what is meant by 'locally available' is, simply, 'not imported' into a country. For the villager, however, anything that is not freely available in the village is effectively an import, whether imported from an urban centre or from a neighbouring country. For villagers seeking to construct any item, the main distinction is between materials which can be acquired for nothing and those which have to be paid for, since the

latter implies greater demands on very limited capital resources.

Pre-processing methods and devices

Some raw materials need to be pre-treated before oil extraction and a range of devices is available for these steps. In some cases presses/expellers are sold as complete units with pre-treatment equipment included, and several manufacturers supply pre-processing equipment. It is necessary to consult appropriate institutions about the suitability of particular machines. If a local agency cannot be found then international agencies such as NRI, GATE or ITDG can be consulted.

Oil-seeds and nuts

Seeds and nuts, in many cases, are heated before processing, although this depends to a large extent on the type of seed or nut and the particular model of expeller being used. Traditionally this heating is carried out over open fires but units known as seed scorchers are now available with a greater degree of temperature control and capable of handling substantially larger quantities of raw material.

Groundnuts

If groundnuts are to be processed using traditional methods then the use of a decorticator to remove the shells before processing will reduce the labour. When processing groundnuts in an expeller, however, the presence of fibre is needed to maintain a suitable operating temperature. The shell may be left on, some shells added, or some residue from a previous batch included to provide fibre for the unit to 'bite' on; otherwise a paste like peanut butter is produced rather than oil. Because of the high fibre in the residual cake when using this method, it can be difficult to sell it in the form of balls or fried cakes (NRI, unpublished information).

Palm kernel nuts

Palm kernel nuts need to be cracked and heated before processing. Crackers which depend on centrifugal force can now be used to replace traditional manual cracking. Both manual and power-driven crackers are available, but verbal communication during the preparation of this book questioned their applicability.

Depending on the type of expeller, the palm kernels may need to be roasted, for example in an oil drum roaster which is hand-rotated over a fire (ILO, 1984). In order for a roaster to be fuel-efficient, its use is recommended only when larger quantities of nuts are being used (ITDG, unpublished information). Finally, oil is extracted from the palm kernel nuts by passing them through an expeller which is described in the following section.

Coconuts

Various types of manual coconut graters are available which are hand- and foot-operated. The design of the scraper blade of the grater (the number and size of grooves) is very important and affects oil yield. The grating stage is tedious and arduous and the use of small motorized graters can ease the work load and also increase oil yields in the traditional oil extraction processes.

If coconuts are to be processed using expellers then the coconut meat needs first to be dried to copra. Prior to oil extraction the particle size must be reduced by chipping or grinding.

Oil extraction devices

Oil expellers

Expellers use a horizontally rotating metal 'screw' which feeds oil-bearing raw material into a barrel-shaped outer casing with perforated walls. Raw material is continuously fed to the expeller which grinds, crushes and presses the oil out as it passes through the machine. The pressure ruptures the oil cells in the raw material, and oil flows through the perforations in the casing and is collected in a trough underneath (GATE, 1979).

The residue of the material from which oil has been extracted exits from the unit, and is known as the 'cake'. With some types of expeller (for example, Cecoco, the Mini 40), the oil-seed or nut may need to be heated before extraction takes place. This allows for greater oil extraction and reduces wear and tear on the machine.

Most small expellers are power-driven, typically requiring about 3 hp, and are able to process between 8 and 45 kg per hour of raw material depending upon the type of expeller used. Bigger units processing greater quantities are available for use in larger mills.

The friction created by the materials being processed wears down the worm shaft and other internal parts. With small machines this occurs often after processing as little as 50 tonnes – after which parts must be replaced or repaired through resurfacing by welding. Maintenance of an oil expeller, therefore, calls for machinery and equipment rarely found in small repair shops, and local manufacture of expellers would be most unlikely at the village/small town level.

Ghanis

Ghanis originated in India where they are primarily used to extract oil from mustard and sesame seeds, although in some cases they can be used for coconut and groundnut. Traditionally ghanis are operated by animals and can be manufactured locally. They consist of a wooden mortar and wood or stone pestle. The mortar is fixed to the ground while the pestle, driven by one or a pair of bullocks (or other draught animals) is located in the mortar where the seeds are crushed by friction and pressure.

The oil runs through a hole at the bottom of the mortar while the residue – or cake – is scooped out. Depending on the size of the mortar and the type of seeds, an animal-powered ghani can process about 10 kg of seeds every two hours (NRI, unpublished information). Normally, two bullocks are needed because the animal tires after three to four hours. These units typically require two or three people to operate. Scarcity of suitable draught animals sometimes results in bullock ghanis being operated by direct human power. Because of the high frictional forces in the extraction process, this requires at least three people, and sometimes as many as six, who will very often be women. The extent of this practice is unknown, but it fortunately appears to be limited (NRI, unpublished material).

Mechanized versions of the traditional animal-powered ghani are becoming increasingly common. In these power-driven ghanis the pestle and mortar units are usually arranged in pairs with either the pestle or mortar held stationary while the other is rotated. Power ghanis have a greater capacity than the traditional and

can process about 100 kg of seed per day (Srikanta Rao, P.V., 1978). In the case of mustard seed, however, most people prefer the flavour of the bullock-ghani oil because its slower rate of extraction means that more flavour develops. Power ghanis yield an oil with a lower pungency.

Oil plate presses

Plate presses are normally used for extracting oil from mesocarp fruits such as oil palm but, depending upon the amount of pressure applied, oil-seeds and nuts can also be processed. These are commonly of two types; screw presses and hydraulic presses.

In a screw press which is manually operated, the substance from which the oil is to be extracted is pressed slowly and with maximum pressure by a plunger (round steel plate), forced down by a screw, and into a cylinder with a large number of small holes (GATE, 1979). Capacities of screw presses depend upon the size of the cage (which holds the product), an average being about 15 kg per batch.

In a hydraulic press, which can be manually or power operated, pressure is exerted by a hydraulic device such as a lorry jack. They require a heavy, rigid frame structure. Because of the weight of such a structure the press must be stationary and cannot be moved as easily as a screw press. Hydraulic presses can process mesocarp fruits, oil-seeds, and nuts as they generate greater pressure than a screw press. A general warning with hydraulic presses: it is essential to ensure that hydraulic fluid, which may be toxic, does not come into contact with the foodstuff (GATE, 1979).

In most cases, oil presses can be manufactured locally in rural areas with the exception of the screw which needs a special lathe (probably found in an industrial area). It is generally recommended that the nut (through which the screw operates) should be of a softer metal so that it will be subject to wear and tear rather than the screw, which is more expensive to replace or repair. Hydraulic presses can be manufactured locally if lorry jacks are available.

Refining

Oil produced in large commercial mills passes through a refining stage which includes neutralization, decolorization, filtration and deodorization. Some of these processes can be adapted for use at the rural level. For example, clarification of oil can be improved by treatment with charcoal or by filtering through cloth or sand. If sand is used, attention should be paid to its quality. Palatability may be improved by boiling. Packaging in well-cleaned and properly closed containers will improve the market value.

Systems for oil processing

From the description of the different traditional oil processing technologies and suggestions for their improvements

discussed so far it can be seen that no general solution applies. Essentially each oil-bearing material has to be considered separately, as do the steps it has to go through during its processing.

Complete package systems are readily available for medium- to large-scale commercial production for particular kinds of oil-bearing material. However, complete packages, suitable for small villages are far less common (although many institutions are engaged in developing equipment which may fill this gap). A book of this size could not begin to cover all the processing methods for the various oil-bearing materials. It has been decided to include one system developed by KIT for palm oil processing in its totality in order to give a better understanding of a complete process (Royal Tropical Institute, unpublished information).

KIT village level palm oil processing system

The process includes the following steps:
o sterilizing and cooking the fruit;
o pounding by hand to loosen pulp from the nuts;
o reheating the pounded material with steam;
o pressing;
o clarifying the oil.

Stage 1 *Sterilization*

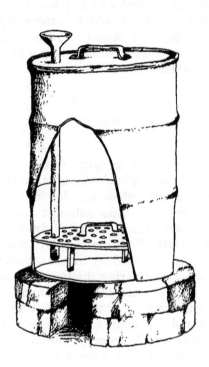

Once the palm fruits have been gathered they are placed in a 'sterilizer' or steamer and cooked. The sterilizer, consisting of an oil drum fitted with a perforated false bottom with water below it, is placed above a fire. Steaming helps loosen the pulp from the nuts during later pounding and also determines, to a considerable extent, the quality of the final palm oil by destroying micro-organisms present and inactivating the enzymes which produce free fatty acids.

Stage 2 *Pounding*

The steamed mixture is then pounded, usually with a mortar and pestle, to strip the pulp from the nuts. Fibre from previous batches is mixed in at this stage to give a greater extraction efficiency during the subsequent pressing step. One observation has shown that it takes four people about 5 minutes to pound 30 kg.

Stage 3 *Reheating with steam*

In order to improve the permeability of the oil-bearing cell walls and so facilitate the removal of oil from the mass, the pulp must be steamed for one hour. A steaming kettle, very similar to the sterilizer, is placed over a fire. Water is added through a funnel to stop the kettle from going dry. During reheating a certain percentage of palm oil will leak out of the pulp and drip through the perforated plate into an oil reservoir which is placed on a tripod above the cooking water.

Stage 4 *Pressing*

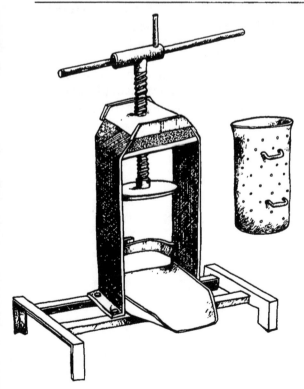

A hand-operated screw press is provided with two cages, each of 17 litres capacity, so that one can be refilled while the other is being pressed. Each reheated batch is divided into three pressing batches and each is then pressed for 10 minutes. The oil recovery by pressing is 90 per cent.

Stage 5 *Clarification*

Next, the crude oil is poured into a clarifier. This consists of a barrel which has a double bottom containing a layer of near boiling water which works as a bain-marie (water bath). During heating over a fire, three layers are formed – pure oil, sludge, and water. The oil floats to the top and is skimmed off using a calabash, then poured into a shallow pan and heated briefly to evaporate all traces of water in it. This improves the keeping quality of the oil. The clarifier is equipped with a tap at the base of the double bottom in order to empty it.

The KIT unit provides one comprehensive system for processing palm oil.

It is worth mentioning that another system is being promoted by APICA (*Association Pour la Promotion des Initiatives Communautaires Africaines*). Although not as detailed as the KIT system, the following information is included. The APICA unit, because its output is greater, is more applicable for use by co-operatives and small plantations. The system consists of a bunch stripper which separates the individual nuts after harvesting. A continuous feed, single screw hand- or mechanically driven Colin press is used for oil-extraction. Colin presses were imported from France particularly to the Cameroons between 1930 and 1960 and APICA now has a programme to recondition these presses. The package also includes a simple clarifying stage using boiling water (ATI, 1984).

4
Case studies

IN VIEW OF the considerable range of technologies for improved traditional extraction and processing of oil, selection of the most appropriate technology for a given environment requires:

o a careful examination of social, economic, technical and environmental factors;
o a thorough review of current technical developments; and
o an analysis of the competitiveness of traditional processing in comparison to the improved methods under given conditions.

Obviously, women will be reluctant to accept new technologies (particularly if they require capital investment) which do not reduce the more arduous aspects of the work and which do not prove to be viable and appropriate to their needs.

Technologies such as oil presses and expellers have normally been introduced with the intention of improving traditional methods. However, many have had limited success because they have tended to ignore considerations such as fuel and water availability. Women haul considerable amounts of fuel and water which are very important to the whole process. For example, the whole process of oil extraction requires 7 kg of fuel in Ghana and 6 kg in Sierra Leone to produce 4 kg of palm oil. If the peak period of production coincides with the dry season, or if enough fuelwood is not available, so-called improved technologies may not provide a viable alternative to traditional methods.

This section seeks to provide examples of the problems encountered in trying to improve traditional methods of processing oil. It points in particular to the dangers of ignoring the strength of traditional technologies and the benefits of trying to build upon them. As previously mentioned, the case studies highlight the need to examine socio-economic relations, such as social organization, ownership and control of resources, and the need to provide support services such as training and credit.

Oil expellers

From the information already collected it would seem that oil expellers are always owned by male entrepreneurs or men's co-operatives and are always operated by men. Women can only take advantage of these if they have the time to walk to the plant and pay for the service either by cash or by leaving some of the seed or oil as payment (Hammonds, T.W. *et al*, 1985).

However, there seems to be no reason why women could not own and operate an expeller on a co-operative basis if given the opportunity to do so.

Oil plate presses

Groundnut oil – Burkina Faso

Screw press

In Burkina Faso, a press was introduced into a US Save the Children Federation project with a view to improving the traditional method of groundnut oil processing. The traditional method of processing groundnuts is similar to the one mentioned in Section 2.

The oil press presented several problems. The small round plate that fits into the cylinder to press the nuts regularly stuck at an angle inside the cylinder, because of uneven pressure caused either by inconsistent chopping of the nuts or by the fact that they were inadequately pounded. The press is only large enough to take about 2 kg of nuts at a time, which does not produce enough oil to make it worth the time and effort. The press is also very heavy, hard to clean, and totally unfamiliar to the women.

Although the press eliminated the operation of skimming oil from the surface, this is one of the easier steps of the whole production process. It would have made much more sense to develop a machine that removes the skin from the grilled nut. This is a slow, labour-intensive process that is still done with a mat and wooden board.

By-products of oil production were not considered. Women made a bigger profit with the traditional method by selling the kuli kuli groundnut cookies than they did from selling the oil itself. The by-product from the oil press was a hard, cake-like mass of chopped nuts that can be used as animal feed, or pounded into powder for cooking sauces. The marketability of this product had not been determined (Corbett, 1981).

Palm oil – Sierra Leone

Screw press

Palm oil production and processing in Sierra Leone is largely carried out by traditional methods. Both men and women are involved. While men harvest the fruit-laden branches, the women's task is to separate (manually) the fruits from the bunches. Crushing the fruit, by treading, is done by both men and women. It is the women's job to transport water to wash the crushed fruits, then they reheat the crude oil to produce pure oil. The demands on women to supply water for processing are considerable. The availability of water is, in fact, the biggest limitation on traditional processing as the peak period of production occurs during the dry season when water is scarce.

Since palm oil processing is an important source of income for rural women, the need to relieve constraints on such processing and increase the productivity of women's labour was identified. Given the tendency for equipment to be designed without consideration of women's requirements, and for men to take over these jobs once new technologies have been introduced, an attempt was made to develop a women-oriented project. The aim was to incorporate women's priorities into the design of the press and then to introduce oil presses directly to groups of village women involved in oil processing. Presses were designed by the Department of Engineering at Fourah Bay College, to the Ministry of Social Welfare's specification and with UN funding. A few prototypes were produced for testing in oil-processing villages.

Although the oil presses were installed in 13 villages, it appears that in many of them little field testing was done. In some cases the villagers simply refused to use the new press; in others, after an initial demonstration they refused to take part in any further trials. In one instance the press became damaged in use, and was never returned from Freetown, where it had been taken for repair. Proper field testing in other villages was difficult owing to a lack of transport for demonstration and monitoring. Furthermore, many presses were introduced during the off-peak season.

In those villages where field testing was carried out, results were not favourable. The machine was reported to be too small; there were no time savings; output was actually lower than that obtained with the traditional method; the machine was not easily operated by women and the process used more fuelwood – a scarce commodity. In total, the new 'improved' press was firmly rejected by the villages in the pilot scheme.

This project, which was designed to incorporate some of the lessons learned from experiences of previous technology and employment projects, itself ran into just as many difficulties. Part of the problem seemed to lie in the lack of communication between social welfare staff and the engineers at the university. The engineers relied entirely on information from social welfare officers who, however, failed to note or pass on relevant information, because they did not understand its importance to the project. Since the engineers had been told that it would be useful for the equipment to be portable, so that it could be moved between villages, they concentrated on this feature and ignored the more important consideration of the normal batch processing size wanted by the villages. They also developed an energy-intensive boiler for use in an area of fuelwood shortage.

Once the prototype had been designed, the university staff were unable to produce the required numbers for testing. Their priorities were to teach and develop new projects, not to manufacture the equipment itself. Most of the presses arrived too late for the main harvest and were delivered to the villages for testing in the off-peak season. Pressure of work and lack of transport also made it difficult for both engineers and social workers to visit test sites, so there was no attempt to modify the prototypes in line with the villagers' responses and reactions.

Even if the prototype had been modified and had proved to be acceptable and useful, no arrangements had been made for scaling up for commercial manufacture and distribution to supply the demand generated.

It was obviously not a job for the university and the design was too complicated for the average rural metal-working shop. In any case, producers of metal goods were experiencing enormous problems in acquiring imported raw materials. This is a classic example of how crucial it is to make sufficiently detailed studies of the technical, economic and socio-cultural aspects of the process to be upgraded. It also demonstrates that, before embarking on a project which aims at generating interest in a new piece of hardware, thought needs to be given as to how large numbers could be produced and disseminated (Carr, 1984).

Palm oil – Tanzania

Screw press

A major problem faced by women with the introduction of new improved technology is the loss of their jobs. In Tanzania, for example, an improved palm oil press was introduced to relieve the women's workload. Although the presses were meant to be hand-operated they required too much strength or could only be operated using animal power. The women found the machines too strenuous to operate and they did not own livestock to operate the press.

Consequently, the men took over the machines and the trade. The women now produce palm oil using traditional methods only for domestic purposes while the men are earning an income using the presses (Tech and Tools, 1986). Income earned by men is not returned to the family purse, whilst women's earnings are normally invested in the family by purchasing items such as food, children's clothes and school tuition.

Palm oil – Senegal

Screw press

In Casamance, Senegal, ENDA (Environment–Development–Action) introduced a screw-type palm oil press consisting of a steel screw spindle turned on a lathe and a cast bronze nut, all made by the village smith. This method ensures that the screw is not subjected to excess wear and the nut can be replaced by a new 'home-made' one at any time. A steel nut would mean increased wear on the screw and could not be replaced on the spot. The advantage of the press is the simplicity of its construction. It is not welded, and all parts are fixed exclusively by means of screws or home-made rivets.

By 1983, 48 presses had been constructed and distributed by village smithies. The project succeeded in achieving a promising improvement in palm oil processing while involving village craftsmen. However, there were marketing difficulties. Many of the villages are remote and difficult to reach, so that the inhabitants are dependent on private traders for the sale of their palm oil. These traders turn up at irregular intervals and purchase the oil at low prices. A marketing strategy should have been better developed in the early stages of the project (Jacobi, 1983).

Palm oil – Ghana

Screw press

In Ghana women produce palm oil for both consumption and soap-making. In the 1970s, because tallow was in short supply, the demand for palm oil in soap manufacture increased. The Technology Consultancy Centre (TCC) therefore investigated ways in which greater quantities of palm oil could be produced at a relatively low cost. If rural extraction methods were improved then palm oil could be used extensively for both consumption and soap-making. The centre succeeded in designing and constructing a hand-operated screw press for the extraction of palm oil by adapting existing

presses being used in Sierra Leone and Nigeria. The press, operated by two people, is capable of pressing 20 kg of pounded boiled fruit at a time. The pressing is done only once, as it has been found that second pressing yields little additional oil and at a high cost. A smaller version of the press has also been developed to take a maximum of 6.8 kg of fruits. The extraction time for each press was 12 minutes.

Since the introduction of the presses, the TCC has also developed a range of equipment which is used with the press. The system consists of a boiling tank, a pounding machine, press, clarifying tank, and storage tank. The mill, which is capable of producing an average of half a tonne of oil per day, is aimed at farmers with plantations ranging between 1 and 150 acres (60 hectares). The introduction of the TCC mini oil mills has made it possible to increase considerably the output of Ghana's small-scale oil palm farmers. Moreover, with the TCC mini mills the farmers can process their own crop. Since the programme started in 1976, approximately 250 oil mills have been established. With an average output of half a tonne of oil per day for 180 days a year, the estimated capacity created through the establishment of the TCC mini oil mills comes to 22 500 tonnes.

Consequently, there has been a marked improvement in the earning power of the indigenous Ghanian oil palm farmer. This increase of the earning power is also reflected in the growth of the Ghanaian palm oil industry as a whole (TCC, unpublished information).

Shea-butter – Mali

Hydraulic press

A new hydraulic hand-press developed by the Royal Tropical Institute in the

Netherlands was tested by GATE/GTZ over two years in four Malian villages. The press is based on the dry method in which fat is squeezed out of heated shea-powder under high pressure.

The new technique consists of four stages: pounding the kernels down to a very fine powder; heating the powder to about 100°C in a pot; keeping it hot for about one hour in a hot-air oven; and finally pressing the hot powder in the hydraulic hand-press. Afterwards, the fat is cleared of all traces of pressing residues by bringing it to the boil together with okra, lemon juice and water. To achieve maximum output, the whole procedure is repeated. The resulting presscake is excellent fuel for ovens and considerably reduces the fuelwood demand.

With the traditional technique the fat output is somewhere between 25 and 40 per cent related to dry kernels. Using the shea-press, a quantity of up to 45 per cent can be attained; the tests in Mali gave an average result of 35 per cent (first and second pressing). The fat amount to be derived is decided, however, by the condition of the raw material. A chemical analysis of the butter manufactured under the new technique did not yield any difference from that produced with the traditional method.

Generally, the heating of the powder to between 100°C and 120°C is not difficult for the women. Operation of the press requires some manual movements such as opening and closing the release valve and unscrewing the jack cylinder; this the women learned to master only after some instruction. In the beginning a lot of problems were faced with the frame of the press which became deformed because of very high pressure. Additionally, the cage was not properly placed. As a result GATE/GTZ conducted training courses for the women using the press. Small technical problems can be handled by these trained women in addition to regular maintenance such as changing the seals of the jacks. However, problems with the lifting jack have to be dealt with by an experienced engineer.

The price of the press is high, and most village women in Mali suffer from a chronic shortage of cash. However, the women realized that, by using the press, they could make a profit which covered the cost of the press in one year.

In each Mali village the women were instructed to operate the press on their own and to acquire some experience with this new technology. Enthusiasm among them was spontaneous. Within a relatively short time and without major effort they were able to produce more shea-butter than they had done with the old technique. Although the women had to take some trouble to handle the press properly, some of them, keen enough to help every day, were soon able to work it without instructions. In one of the villages this know-how was passed on without any problems. However, rivalries emerged among the women because each family clan tried, even at the expense of others, to look after its own interests. The dispute about who would be given authority to operate the new technology surfaced even during the test phase.

There is also the danger that the machine could bring about a change in the traditional division of labour, with adverse effects for women. Since the press can quite easily be used to produce groundnut oil, and since groundnuts are traditionally traded by men, new income earning possibilities also emerge for them. A second danger is that the shea-butter could become a mere cash crop. The traditional system of solidarity – whereby a woman pays the helping women by giving them some shea-butter

– could break down in favour of selling all the butter (Niess, 1983).

Alternative energy sources

Micro-hydro oil mills – Nepal

In Nepal, oil-seeds (especially mustard) were traditionally processed with a kol – a heavy timber rotated in a hollowed-out boulder containing the seed. The process is arduous and time-consuming, and yields relatively little oil. Diesel-powered mills were introduced to replace the kols, but these proved to be expensive.

In the late 1970s, micro-hydro plants were installed with processing equipment for flour mills, rice mills and 'baby' oil expellers. The use of water-powered mills in the mountains of Nepal has permitted more efficient exploitation of an indigenous resource to process grains and oil-seeds at village level.

Micro-hydro plants are less costly to maintain and operate then diesel plants. Because the technology was already well understood, they were easy to install and maintain. As the plants are being introduced rapidly and are widely accepted, small workshops in the area are becoming aware of the technology and are fabricating some of the machinery. By 1986, 450 turbines had been installed, and sites and finance for a further 450 had been identified. According to an evaluation study, each household using a mill was saving between 800 and 3000 person-hours each year. Most of the labour time saved is that of unpaid female and child labour within the household. The time now made available is said to be taken up with improved child and livestock care, more fodder gathering and household chores (Hislop, 1987).

Technology change to meet women's choice

Change from dry to wet method of oil extraction – Philippines

Coconuts are abundant in the area surrounding the village of Oguis in Misamis Oriental in the Philippines. In 1983, with the help of the parish priest and the Xavier University extension service, the villagers established a 500-nuts-a-day coconut oil extraction plant. The community, especially the women, joined together to build this plant, contributing their labour for the construction and assisted by a loan from the Ramon Aboitiz Foundation Incorporated (RAFI).

The plant originally operated using the dry method. Coconuts were husked, cut in half and the meat removed from the shell to be flue-dried to produce good quality copra. Then the copra was cut with knives, mostly by women, and fed to a crusher before it was pressed. The crusher and the press required a great deal of strength and this stage was done by men. Then the oil was refined by steaming – a long, hot process, again delegated to women, along with soap-making which entailed the dangers of working with corrosive sodium hydroxide. Daily, the plant produced 2.5 kg of charcoal, 24 litres of edible oil, 30 bars of soap and some 50 kg of copra meal.

The plant ran into several problems during its operation. The machines broke down so often that they held up operation, and a lack of peace and order in the village prevented the villagers from working constantly. It was also found that the plant did not make use of the nutritive value of coconuts. Since the plant used relatively heavy machines it had to employ mostly men.

In 1985 the plant had to be abandoned

because the villagers evacuated to the town centres following worsening clashes between the rebel and the military groups in the village. All this time they remained as a community and thought of ways in which they could improve the utility and efficiency of the coconut processing plant. Together with the Appropriate Technology Centre of the College of Agriculture Complex at Xavier University, the women of the village decided to change from the dry method to the more traditional wet method of oil extraction.

The wet method, as described in Section 2, would confer more advantages to the women of the village of Oguis. First, this is the method they had been used to, but made more efficient. Second, besides edible oil, soap and charcoal, it would produce coagulated protein as a dietary supplement for children and cocomeal feed for hogs. Women would therefore benefit from the supplementary income. Third, this plant could employ mostly women because the machinery involved would be much lighter and easier to operate (Xavier University, unpublished information).

Summary

In introducing new technologies it is important to make comparisons between the proposed improved technology and traditional methods. The case studies show that various issues need to be considered before introducing equipment. In some cases, it was found that the new technology was no better than the traditional method and, in fact, increased the labour requirements and time inputs or resulted in an excessive demand for raw materials.

The availability of inputs such as animal power and human power need to be assessed. In Sierra Leone one of the reasons why the press was inappropriate was that it required greater amounts of water and fuel – which were already scarce. In cases like this, or in areas where diesel and electricity are unavailable, alternative energy sources should be considered for powering the oil mills.

The degree of complexity of equipment and its maintenance requirements are also important. If women are unable to maintain the equipment, or if spare parts are not easily accessible, then the technology will be of little use.

Care should always be taken that the new technology is financially viable. Women should be able to afford the technology or have access to credit. The technology should pay for itself in a given time through sale of its products and even create a secondary enterprise by making use of the by-products. This is especially true of oil processing where the cake by-product can be sold as a constituent of livestock feed.

Even if a technology is financially viable, there is still a danger that it will have an adverse affect on women by depriving them of their income. In Tanzania, for example, it was the men who profited from the use of a new palm oil press rather than the women. Thus, again, it is essential to place the problem in the context of the total village system, taking into account technical, economic, social, and cultural factors. For example, do the people like to work co-operatively; who owns the raw materials; who has control of the marketing mechanisms? By examining the village system first and placing the 'problem' within it, you are more likely to identify important constraints and preconditions to the successful introduction of any technical change. A careful study of these factors can help to determine which of the various stages of oil processing require improvements offering maximum benefits to the intended beneficiaries.

5
Planning a project or enterprise

FROM the selection of case studies presented in Section 4, some questions emerge which should be asked by project planners and decision makers before they proceed with the implementation of an oil processing project or promotion of an oil extraction enterprise.

Some questions, particularly socio-economic issues, are of fundamental importance and must be addressed in baseline data or feasibility studies at the initial stages of project planning. Looking at the questions below may draw attention to areas where more information is needed before project implementation can go ahead. Other questions, particularly those concerned purely with technical information, may be answered (having carried out the initial studies) with simple one- or two-sentence or yes/no answers.

The first questions are concerned with the viability of the enterprise; then there are questions about the role of women in traditional processing, with subsidiary questions listed below the main question where appropriate; and finally the impact of improved technologies is considered.

First questions

1. Why set up a small-scale oil processing venture?
   ○ Is there a market for increased yields?
   ○ Can the existing system cope with increased demand?
   ○ If yes to the above, how will you improve/add capacity?
2. When processing a given quantity of fruit, nuts or oil-seeds using the traditional process, what inputs are required?
   ○ How much time is required?
   ○ What is the labour input required by male and female labour for each activity or stage?
   ○ How much fuel is used, and is it readily available?
   ○ How much oil is yielded?
   ○ What is the value of the inputs (raw materials, fuel, water, packaging) in comparison with the output?

Background questions

1. What exactly is the place of women in traditional processing? What role do they play in the different stages?
   ○ What is the traditional marketing mechanism and who controls it? (Do women have access to markets?)

    ○ What proportion of the income from the processed oil do women earn and keep?
    ○ What are the major problems and difficulties of women producers in this field?

2. What is the extent of traditional and small-scale oil processing in the area?
    ○ What is the traditional process?
    ○ Are there different traditional methods of processing the oil?   Yes ☐   No ☐
    ○ Which method tends to be used most frequently, and why?
    ○ Does the main method vary in different parts of the country?

(It is important to know about the various traditional methods being used, as this may influence the improvements needed.)

3. Who owns the raw materials?
    ○ Are there more raw materials available than can be processed in the traditional manner?   Y ☐   N ☐
    ○ Are there ever seasonal shortages of raw materials?   Y ☐   N ☐
    ○ What is done with the by-products?

Effect of improved technology on traditional processing industry

Technical considerations

1. Will the use of the improved technology reduce labour input as compared with the traditional method? How?
2. What is the capacity of the improved technology – will it be able to cope with the demands of processing in terms of quantity of material available to processors?
3. Will the equipment produce a greater quantity and better quality of oil than traditional means? (Will the oil have a different taste – if so, will it be acceptable?)
4. What will be the extraction rate of the oil?
5. Will the process be faster? Y ☐   N ☐
6. What are the water/fuel/power requirements of the equipment?
7. Will the users be able to meet those requirements? Y ☐   N ☐
8. Will use of the equipment require a change in packaging Y ☐   N ☐ or transport of the material? Y ☐   N ☐
9. If power-driven equipment is being introduced, can the users meet the electrical/diesel requirements on a regular basis? Y ☐   N ☐
10. Are there alternative energy sources? Y ☐   N ☐
11. Are there means of producing equipment and/or spares locally? Y ☐   N ☐
12. Can the equipment be maintained using local resources?
    ○ are spare parts available? Y ☐   N ☐
    ○ can local artisans repair the machinery Y ☐   N ☐, or do they need to be trained Y ☐   N ☐?
13. Will the users be able to afford the cost of spare parts? Y ☐   N ☐
14. Will the users of the equipment need to be trained?
    ○ will they need technical training Y ☐   N ☐ and if so, how much?
    ○ is training locally available? Y ☐   N ☐
    ○ is there already some familiarity with this type of technology? Y ☐   N ☐

Socio-economic considerations

1. What is the cost of the machine and related equipment?
2. Is the cost manageable on an individual or community basis?
3. If credit is needed is it accessible? Will the women be able to repay the loan?
4. What will the return on the investment be? What will the monthly profit be?
5. How many years will it take the operator to cover the cost of the machine?
6. Who will control use of the machine? Will it be co-operatively controlled or will individual men or women manage it?
7. Who will earn the income after processing?
8. Will availability of the improved technology increase women's income generation?
    o if not, why not?
    o what proportion of the income would women earn?
    o would oil processing remain a significant income generating activity for women after introduction of the machine?
9. Will introduction of the equipment bring about any change in the pattern of work and work habits? How?
    o male
    o female
10. Will there be a change in the daily schedule required to do any task?
11. Does the improved equipment require more or less raw material than traditional methods?
12. If it requires more, is that supply available and who owns it?
13. Will the improved method change the traditional market mechanisms?
14. If more oil is processed, can the market cope with the increase and will this affect the price?
15. What will happen to the by-products from the improved method?
16. If by-products are sold who will earn the income?
17. Will the users be able to cope with the consequential requirements of effective enterprise development such as handling employees, market and price negotiations, and cash flow?

6

Pre-processing and extraction equipment: facts and figures

THIS SECTION aims to give an informed guide to the range of improved devices available for use in oil extraction projects/enterprises within each category described in Section 3. The differences between expellers, ghanis and plate presses are explained in that section.

A. Pre-processing equipment
- ○ Groundnut decorticator
- ○ Coconut grater
- ○ Heater
- ○ Palm nut roaster

B. Expellers
- ○ Caltech/Colin press
- ○ Komet spindle press
- ○ Cecoco press
- ○ Mini 40

C. Ghanis
- ○ Traditional animal-powered
- ○ Power-driven

D. Plate presses:
Screw presses
- ○ TCC press
- ○ KIT spindle press

Hydraulic presses
- ○ KIT press
- ○ KIT press

A range of available equipment is described to suit various needs and circumstances. Where possible, details are given on the price range*, size, capacity, skill level and manufacturing requirements of each piece of equipment. This is aimed at helping consultants/project managers to decide whether a device exists which is appropriate to local needs and circumstances, and helping them to converse on more equal terms with the technologists who are needed to supply the technical solutions.

Although only a limited number of machines are described here, they are carefully chosen to indicate the range available. It should be stressed that before ordering any equipment it would be beneficial to consult appropriate institutions (listed in the Contacts section), especially those who have had previous experience in introducing the equipment. It is noted that all of the expellers and presses will need spare parts for regular replacement as they perform abrasive work.

The following table summarizes the pretreatment and extraction equipment together with the use of the residues (TPI, 1971). This summary table is followed by an illustrated guide of selected equipment with fuller details where available.

* Price codes are taken from *Small-Scale Food Processing* (1992) and are as follows: 1 = up to US$170; 2 = US$171–850; 3 = US$851–1700; 4 = more than US$1700.

Product	Pre-treatment	Extraction equipment	Secondary product uses
Oil-seeds			
Castor		Ghani, Expeller/ Hydraulic press	Cake – fertilizer
Linseed/ Niger	Heated	" "	Cake – livestock feed
Sesame/ Sunflower		" "	Cake – fertilizer, livestock feed
Mustard/Rape		" "	Cake – restricted use to ruminants
Nuts			
Coconuts	Dried and chopped	Expeller/ Hydraulic press	Ropes, fuel, livestock feed
Groundnuts	Decorticated and heated	Screw press, Expeller/ Hydraulic press	Cake – livestock feed
Palm kernel nuts	Heated	Expeller	Cake – livestock feed
Shea-nuts	Kernels broken and heated	Expeller/ Hydraulic press	Cake – livestock feed supplement
Mesocarps			
Oil palm	Bunches heated and stripped	Screw press	

Illustrated guide

Pre-processing

Groundnut decorticator

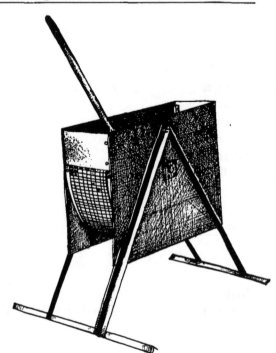

Capacity: 20–30 kg/h.
Operated by loading groundnuts into the trough and moving the paddle backwards and forwards, cracking the groundnut shells against the mesh. The shelled nuts fall through the mesh into a receptacle placed underneath. Can be manufactured in local workshops (UNICEF).

Coconut grater

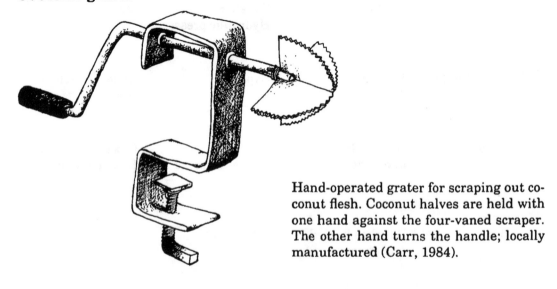

Hand-operated grater for scraping out coconut flesh. Coconut halves are held with one hand against the four-vaned scraper. The other hand turns the handle; locally manufactured (Carr, 1984).

Heater

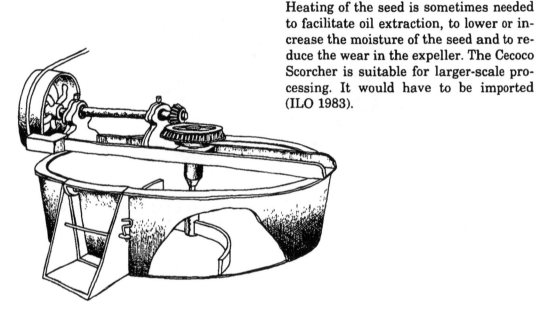

Heating of the seed is sometimes needed to facilitate oil extraction, to lower or increase the moisture of the seed and to reduce the wear in the expeller. The Cecoco Scorcher is suitable for larger-scale processing. It would have to be imported (ILO 1983).

Palm nut cracker

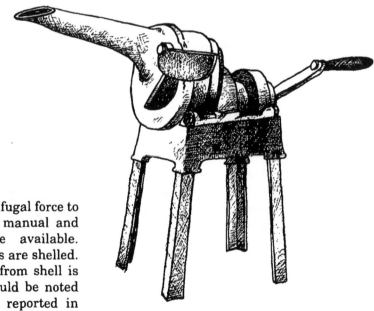

Capacity: 150–200 kg/h

Palm nut crackers use centrifugal force to crack the palm nuts. Both manual and power-driven crackers are available. About 95 per cent of the nuts are shelled. Manual separation of nuts from shell is required (ILO 1984). It should be noted that difficulties have been reported in using some palm nut crackers in field situations.

Palm nut roaster

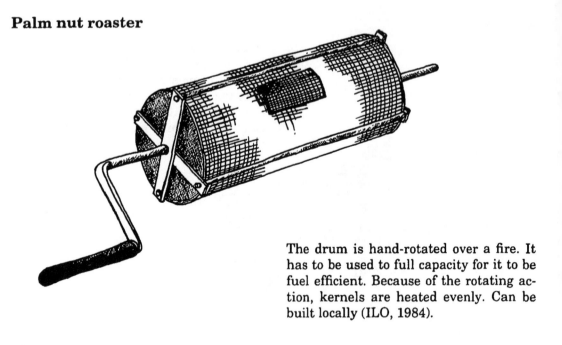

The drum is hand-rotated over a fire. It has to be used to full capacity for it to be fuel efficient. Because of the rotating action, kernels are heated evenly. Can be built locally (ILO, 1984).

Expellers

Caltech/Colin press

Processes: Palm oil fruit
Power source: Manual/power
Capacity: 310 kg/h diesel; 163 kg/h manual
Suitable: Small scale/co-operative
Price code: 4
Manufacture requirements: Castings or fabrication, machining
Skill level: Fairly sophisticated for fabrication
Comments: Works on same principle as expeller; different from screw press because it operates on a continuous feed system which macerates fruit and extracts oil at the same time (APICA, unpublished information). The Caltech press is adapted for small-scale village plantations, while a similar press, the Colin, is used for large-scale plantations.

Note: Price codes are explained on page 24.

Komet spindle press

Processes: Oil-seeds, nuts
Power source: Manual/power
Capacity: 2–5 kg/h manual 8–15 kg/h power
Suitable: Small-scale/large-scale farmer
Price code: Manual 3, powered 4
Manufacture requirements: Castings, machining, fabrication
Skill level: Sophisticated
Comments: Works as an expeller, manual expeller pictured here. However, it is laborious. Some seeds do not need to be heated before expelling; kernels, nuts, copra need to be broken down first. However, it is heavy to operate. A Komet crusher to break down materials is also available. The manufacturer offers a range of expellers to suit needs (*Small-Scale Food Processing*, 1992).

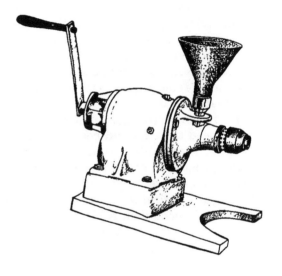

Cecoco press

Processes: Oil-seeds, nuts
Power source: Diesel and electric
Capacity: 30–50 kg/h
Suitable: Large-scale farmer/co-operative
Price code: 3
Manufacture requirements: Castings, machining, fabrication
Skill level: Very sophisticated
Comments: Barrel composed of bars. Some seeds need to be heated before expelling, but does not process copra as readily as the Mini 40, overleaf (*Tools for Agriculture*, 1992 and unpublished information, NRI).

Mini 40

Processes: Oil-seeds, nuts
Power source: Diesel and electric
Capacity: 45–65 kg/h
Suitable: Large-scale farmer/co-operative
Price code: 4
Manufacture requirements: Castings, machining, fabrication
Skill level: Very sophisticated

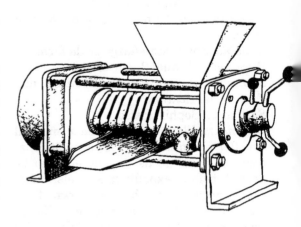

Comments: Barrel composed of rings which need replacing – rings can be made in industrialized area, in a foundry with experience in castings, or imported; seeds do not need to be heated because expelling action generates heat – but this means greater wear and tear on equipment; groundnuts processed with shells (*Tools for Agriculture*, 1992 and unpublished information, NRI).

Ghanis

Traditional animal-powered

Processes: Oil-seeds, nuts
Power source: Animal
Capacity: Average of 40 kg/day; but can vary
Suitable: Small-scale and/or large farmer
Price code: 1 (plus animals)

Manufacture requirements: Carpentry
Skill level: Traditional carpentry
Comments: Capacities vary depending on size and strength of cows and ghani; need two cows because the animal tires after three to four hours (Srikanta Rao, 1978).

Power-driven

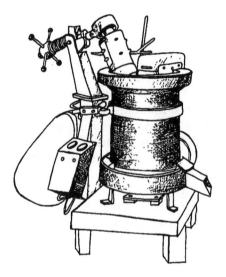

Processes: Oil-seeds, nuts
Power source: 1.5 kW motor
Capacity: 12–15 kg per charge (several charges per day)
Suitable: Large-scale farmer
Price code: 3
Manufacture requirements: Castings, machining, fabrication
Skill level: Sophisticated
Comments: Also known as rotary oil mills: in power ghanis either pestle or mortar remains stationary while the other rotates (*Tools for Agriculture,* 1992).

Screw presses

TCC press

Processes: Palm oil mesocarps
Power source: Manual
Capacity: Depends on size of cage
Suitable: Small-scale farmer
Price code: 2
Manufacture requirements: Fabrication, machining, special lathe for screw
Skill level: Fairly sophisticated
Comments: The illustration gives a good idea of how a screw press works. TCC press is based on this type of model and processes about 20 kg per load. Needs two people to operate (TCC, 1978).

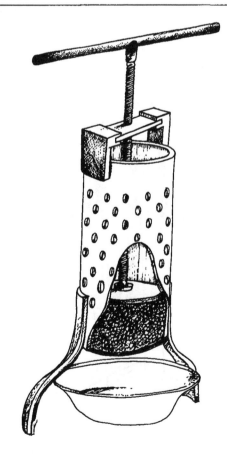

KIT spindle press

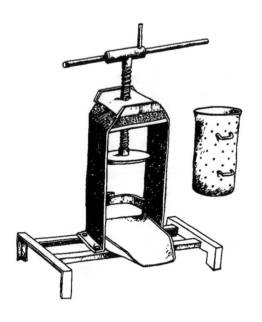

Processes: Palm oil mesocarps
Power source: Manual
Capacity: Small model 4.5 kg per press; large model 9 kg per press
Suitable: Small-scale/larger press for co-operative use
Price code: 3
Manufacture requirements: Machining, fabrication, special lathe for screw
Skill level: Fairly sophisticated
Comments: KIT is trying to develop a press that can press oil-seeds as well (Royal Tropical Institute).

Hydraulic presses

KIT press

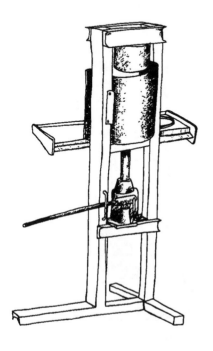

Processes: Oil-seeds, nuts, mesocarps
Power source: Manual
Capacity: 1–2 kg per press
Suitable: Small-scale farmer
Price code: 4
Manufacture requirements: Machining, fabrication
Skill level: Fair degree of welding and fabrication skills
Comments: Because it generates high pressure, seeds do not need to be heated first, but heating will increase oil yield; presses with greater capacities are available; hydraulic jacks from lorries can be used (Royal Tropical Institute).

KIT press

Processes: Shea-nuts, groundnuts
Power source: Manual
Capacity: 5 kg per press
Suitable: Small-scale farmer/co-operative
Price code: 4
Manufacture requirements: Machining, fabrication
Skill level: Fair degree of welding and fabrication skills
Comments: Hydraulic jacks from lorries can be used (Royal Tropical Institute).

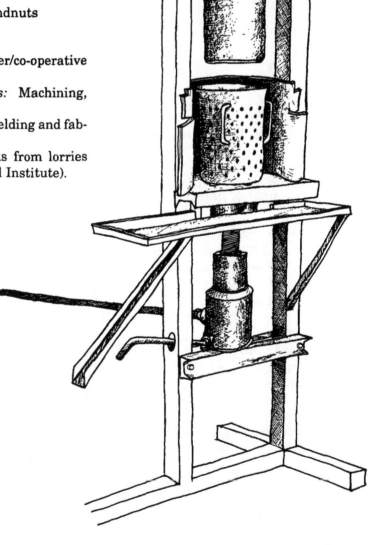

References and further reading

References

ATI (1984)
Annual Report

Carr, M. (1984)
Blacksmith, Baker, Roofing Sheet Maker. IT Publications, London.

Corbett, S. (1981)
'A New Oil Press Design: But is it any better?' *Vita News*, Vita Publications, Washington DC.

ECA (1983)
Traditional Palm Oil Processing: Women's Role and the Application of Appropriate Technology. ATRCW Research Series, Ethiopia.

FAO (1968)
Coconut Oil Processing. Rome.

Fellows, P. and Hampton, A. (1992)
Small-Scale Food Processing: A guide to appropriate equipment. IT Publications, London.

Fleury, J.M. (1981)
The Butter Tree. IDRC Reports, vol. 10, No. 2, IDRC Publications, Ottawa.

GATE (1979)
Oil Presses: An Introduction. GATE/GTZ Publications, Eschborn, Germany.

Hammonds, T.W. Harris, R.V. MacFarlane, N. (1985)
'The Small-Scale Expelling of R.V. Sunflowerseed Oil in Zambia', *Appropriate Technology Journal* vol. 12, No. 1, IT Publications, London.

Hislop, D. (1987)
The Micro-hydro Programme in Nepal – a Case Study, paper presented at IIED Conference on Sustainable Development, London, April 1987.

ILO (1984)
Improved Village Technology for Women's Activities – A Manual for West Africa. ILO Publications, Geneva.

ILO (1983)
Small-Scale Oil Extraction from Groundnuts and Copra. ILO Publications, Geneva.

Jacobi, Carola (1983)
'Palm-Oil Processing with Simple Presses'. *GATE Magazine,* GATE/GTZ Publications, Eschborn, Germany.

Niess, Thomas (1983)
'New Shea-butter Technology for West African Women'. *GATE Magazine,* GATE/GTZ Publications, Eschborn, Germany.

Srikanta Rao, P.V. (1978)
A Search for Appropriate Technology for the Village Oil Industry. ATDA Publications, Lucknow, India.

TCC (1978)
Extraction of Palm Oil Using Appropriate Technology Hand Screw Press. Technology Consultancy Centre Report, Ghana.

TDRI (1984)
Oil Palm News, No. 28.

Tech and Tools (1986)
The Tech and Tools Book: A guide to the technologies women are using worldwide. IT Publications, London.

Tools for Agriculture (1992)
Tools for Agriculture: A guide to appropriate equipment for smallholder farmers. IT Publications, London.

TPI (1971)
Oil and Oilseeds, Crop and Product Digests No. 1, London.

UNICEF
Appropriate Village Technology for Basic Services, Nairobi.

Further reading

Bangor, J., Velasco, J.R.
Coconut Production and Utilization. Philippine Coconut Research and Development Foundation Centre (PCRDF), Amber Avenue, Pasig, Metro Manila, Philippines.

Bowen, B.H. (1976)
A Screw Press for Low-Cost Palm Oil Extraction. Engineering Research Publications; Research Paper No. TE12, published by Univ. of Sierra Leone, Freetown, Sierra Leone.

Bulk, J.V.D. (1986)
Unata Presse, No. 4, Heuvelstraat 131, 3140 Ramsel, Belgium.

Carr, M. (1985)
The A T Reader. IT Publications, London.

Cole, M.J.A., Dr Hamilton, D.B.
Indigenous Technology in Sierra Leone, UNECA/UNICEF.

Donkor, Peter. (1979)
'A Hand-operated Screw Press for Extracting Palm Oil.' *Appropriate Technology,* Vol. 5, No. 4.

Hammond, Terry. (1985)
'The Small-scale Expelling of Sunflower Oil in Zambia.' *Appropriate Technology,* Vol. 12, no. 1.

GRET (1984)
Le Point sur L'Extraction des Huiles Vegetales. GRET Publications, Paris.

German Adult Education Association.
Make Your Own Oil. Africa Bureau. Ghana (traditional palm oil processing)

ILO (1983)
Small-scale Oil Extraction from Groundnuts and Copra. Geneva.

Ihekoronye, R.I., Ngoddy, P.O. (1985)
Integrated Food Science and Technology for the Tropics. MacMillan Publications, London.

McSweeney, Brenda (1982)
'Time to Learn for Women in Upper Volta'. *Appropriate Technology Journal,* Vol. 9, No. 3, IT Pubs, London.

Nwanze, S.C. (1965)
The Hydraulic Hand Press. Nigerian Institute for Oil Palm Research, 4 (15).

Stephens, A. (1986)
Yes, Technology is Gender Neutral, but . . ., CERES 108.

Srikanta Rao, P.V. (1980)
A Search for an Appropriate Technology for Village Oil. ATDA Publications. Lucknow, India.

TCC (1978)
Extraction of Palm Oil Using Appropriate Technology Hand Screw Press. Technology Consultancy Centre Report, Ghana.

TDRI (1983/4)
Oil Palm News, NRI Publications, Chatham.

TPI (1973)
Processing of Oil Palm Fruit and Its Products. TPI Publications, London.

TPI (1973)
An Economic Study of Lauric Oilseed Processing. TPI Publications, London.

TPI (1981)
Rural Technology Guide 10, *A Hand-operated Bar Mill for Decorticating Sunflower Seed*. TPI Publications, London.

TPI (1981)
Rural Technology Guide 9, *A Hand-operated Disc Mill for Decorticating Sunflower Seed*. TPI Publications, London.

Tinker, I.
New Technologies for Food Chain Activities. USAID Paper.

Contacts

The following can be contacted for further information about oil presses and planning oil-press projects. Some of these institutions have developed their own equipment which has been or is being used in the field.

ʻAPICA
Association pour la promotion des initiatives communautaires africaines, BP 7397, Douala-Bussa, Cameroon

ATC
Appropriate Technology Centre, College of Agriculture Complex, Xavier University, Cagayan de Oro City, Philippines 8401

ATDA
Appropriate Technology Development Association, PO Box 311, Gandhi Bhawan, Mahatma Gandhi Road, Lucknow 226001, India

ATI
Appropriate Technology International, 1331 H Street N.W., Washington DC 20005, USA

CAMERTEC
Centre for Agricultural Mechanisation & Rural Technology, PO Box 764, Arusha, Tanzania

CENEEMA
Centre National d'Etudes et d'Expérimentation du Machinisme Agricole, BP 1040 – Yaoundé, Cameroon

ENDA
Environment-Development-Action, BP 3370, Dakar, Senegal

GATE/GTZ
German Appropriate Technology Exchange, Postfach 5180, D-6236 Eschborn 1, Germany

GRET
Groupe de Recherche et d'Echanges Technologiques, 213 rue Lafayette, 75010, Paris, France

ITDG
Intermediate Technology Development Group, Myson House, Railway Terrace, Rugby, UK

KIT
Royal Tropical Institute, Mauritskade 63, 1092 AD Amsterdam, Netherlands

NIFOR
Nigerian Institute for Oil Palm Research, PMB 1, Benin City, Nigeria

NRI
Natural Resources Institute; formerly known as the Tropical Development and Research Institute (TDRI), Central Avenue, Chatham Maritime, Chatham ME4 4TB, UK

TCC
Technology Consultancy Centre, University of Science and Technology, Kumasi, Ghana

United Nations Agencies

The following United Nations agencies are able to offer information on various aspects of oil processing and/or have had experience in oil processing projects.

FAO
Food and Agriculture Organization
Via delle Terme di Caracalla
00100 Rome
Italy

ILO
International Labour Office
CH-1211 Geneva 22
Switzerland

www.ingramcontent.com/pod-product-compliance
Lightning Source LLC
Jackson TN
JSHW052134131224
75386JS00037B/1271